L I L L E N A S® D R A M A

Christmas Program Builder No. 63
Creative Resources for Program Directors

Compiled by Kim Messer

PUBLISHING COMPANY

PO Box 419527
Kansas City, MO 64141

Questions? Please write or call:
Lillenas Publishing Company
Drama Resources
P. O. Box 419527
Kansas City, MO 64141
Phone: 816-931-1900 * Fax: 816-412-8390
Email: drama@lillenas.com
Web Site: www.lillenasdrama.com

Cover Design by Doug Bennett
Executive Editor: Kim Messer
Supervising Editor: Kimberly Meiste
Manuscript Formatting: Karen Phillips

Contents

Recitations for Preschool

Hope

Once a tired earth
Lay bleak and forlorn,
But *hope* came alive
When Jesus was born.

Dorothy Heibel

Christmas Time Love

May God's wonderful
Christmas time love,
Shine down upon us
From heaven above.

Robert Colbert

In a Manger

Baby Jesus was born to Mary
In a manger stall.
But wise men who came to
worship Him
Knew He would be *King* of all!

Dorothy Heibel

Come Let's Hurry

(For two children dressed as shepherds.)
CHILD 1: Come let's hurry
To Bethlehem
Where Christ the
Lord is born,
CHILD 2: And welcome Him
Into our hearts
This happy
Christmas morn.

Robert Colbert

At Christmas

Christmas Day
Is on its way,
Prepare for holidays *bright*!
With prayers to Baby Jesus
Who is
Our *Holy Light*!

Dorothy Heibel

Recitations for Ages 5 to 7

Angel Choirs Sing

The heavens ring with an angel
    choir
Singing as one *grand voice*:
    "He is born, the Holy One!
    Let all the earth rejoice!"

                Dorothy Heibel

This Happy Day

Shepherd's hurried
To see the One
Born this happy day;
Born to bring
Us back to God,
And take our sins away.
Happy Jesus time!

                Robert Colbert

No Gift or Money

(Child puts hands in pockets;
removes them to show audience
that they are empty.)
I have no gift
    Or money,
But there's something
    I can do;
Wish a hearty
    Merry Christmas
To every one of you.
    (Shouting) Merry Christmas!

                Robert Colbert

The Christmas Season

The Christmas season comes again
    As carols fill the air,
And bells ring out the Good News:
    It's time to love and share.

                Dorothy Heibel

Love

God, the Father, sent His Son,
A holy Babe to adore.
He was a never-ending gift
Of *love* forevermore!

                Dorothy Heibel

The First Christmas

Jesus entered the world
From heaven above
To show man how to live
In forgiveness and love.

                Dorothy Heibel

A Holy Gift

Angels sang alleluias
On that first Christmas night.
Shepherds in the hillsides
Beheld a glorious light.
What was the reason?
It's easy to see: *Baby Jesus*
    God's gift
      To you and to me!

                Dorothy Heibel

A Royal Birth

All the earth listens
While angels sing
Of the glorious birth:
Baby Jesus, our King!

                    Dorothy Heibel

A Holy Birth

Jesus, Son of Mary,
Was worshipped at His birth.
He was, and is, and shall be,
God's *greatest gift* to earth.

                    Dorothy Heibel

Christmas Greeting

*(Child holds card in hand
as if reading it.)*
This little Christmas greeting
Comes just now to say;
"Let's all give thanks to God,
For Jesus on Christmas day!"

                    Robert Colbert

Recitations for Ages 8 to 10

Shine

*(Use this at the end of a
Christmas Eve service,
then sing* Silent Night.*)*
Star light,
Star bright,
Bring us peace
This blessed night.
Shine o'er the
Christ Child's manger lowly
And bless the tiny Babe
Most holy!

Dorothy Heibel

Long Ago

The sky was full of
Twinkling stars
On that important night.
But one star shone
The brightest,
Giving off a brilliant light.
It led seekers to
A manger bed
Where the baby Jesus lay.
And still we follow Jesus
Because we know
He is the way!

Dorothy Heibel

Fill Our Hearts

May the bright light
        That shines
From heaven to earth,
        Lead us to our
Savior's birth,
        And fill our hearts
With peace and love,
        The kind that comes
From God above.

Robert Colbert

Bethlehem

Mary and Joseph
Went to Bethlehem
Where Jesus was born
On this earth.

We remember
His humble beginning
And give thanks to God
For His birth.

Dorothy Heibel

Adult Readings and Recitations

Christmas

Christmas is coming!
   It's almost here.
It's the best time
   Of the year!

We give gifts
   And get them too,
Fun for me and
   Fun for you!

But wait!
   Is that what it's all about?
Many gifts
   We could do without!

But one gift is good
   The whole year through:
The Christ Child's love
   Ever loyal and true!

Dorothy Heibel

The Christmas Window

Smiling faces in the window
Holly and bells,
The Star of Bethlehem,
Tiny hand praying,
A Christmas blessing.

Bless the baby Jesus,
Bless the Child of light,
Born in a stable
On this holy night.

Shepherds stand watchful
With donkey and sheep,
Wise men bear presents,
Angels sing peace.
Joseph gives praise,
Mary cradles Jesus,
Jesus gently sleeps.

Smiling faces in the window,
Holly and bells,
The star of Bethlehem,
Tiny hands praying
A Christmas blessing.

Bless the baby Jesus,
Bless the Child of light.
Sweet dreams, baby Jesus
Baby Jesus, noel, noel, noel.

Richard G. Chur

Service

Beyond December—Christmas Eve

by Rick Paashaus

Scripture References: Isaiah 9:2, 49:9, 59:9, 60:1-2; Luke 1:46-69, 2:1-20; John 1:1-14, 8:12

Cast:
- READER 1—Male/Female
- READER 2—Male/Female
- FEMALE READER—Mary
- MALE READER—Joseph
- SCRIPTURE READER
- WORSHIP LEADER/PASTOR

(Scripture references are listed but are not intended to be read.)

READER 1: In the beginning . . . darkness. Genesis 1 tells us that in the beginning, the earth was formless and empty; darkness was over the face of the deep. Darkness . . . I hate the darkness.

READER 2: Job talked about a place of deepest night, of deep shadow and disorder, where even the light is like darkness. Isaiah spoke of the people who walked in darkness . . . stumbling, falling, fearful.

READER 1: I remember when I was little. Mom would tuck me in and I'd say my prayers. But when she left the room, the darkness surrounded me. In the night my little mind raced. Every sound was a monster. Every shadow in the bedroom was coming to get me. Every bad thought or wrong act I had done all day came sweeping over me . . . and I felt so alone. My, how I hated the darkness.

READER 2: In the darkness we lose our grasp on what is true, what is real, what is good. Like the moment the power goes out . . . everyone stops dead in their tracks and waits in silence . . . waiting in uncertainty . . . waiting in fear . . . waiting in the darkness. Isaiah knew that darkness. Listen to his thoughts:

See, darkness covers the earth and thick darkness is over the peoples. Justice is far from us, and righteousness does not reach us. We look for light, but all is darkness; for brightness, but we walk in deep shadows. (Isaiah 59:9, 60:2)

But . . . ah . . . what a precious word . . . "but" . . . The people walking in darkness have seen a great light; on those living in the land of the shadow of death a light has dawned. (Isaiah 9:2)

And when that Light comes, the darkness will be gone. Out of gloom and darkness the eyes of the blind will see. He will turn the darkness into light before them. He will say to the captives, "Come out!" and to those in darkness, "Be free!" (Isaiah 49:9)

And Jesus said, "I am the light of the world. Whoever follows me will never walk in darkness, but will have the light of life." (John 8:12) *Arise! Shine! For the Light has come!* (Isaiah 60:1)

Hymn: "Angels, from the Realms of Glory" (Verses 1, 2, 3, and 5; project white words on a black screen)

Prayer

Mary's Song

Hymn: "What Child Is This?" (All verses; instruments as needed, but gentle)

Female Reader: Who am I? An everyday girl from an ordinary family living in a tiny village in northern Israel . . . not Jerusalem or Antioch or Damascus . . . people used to say, "Can anything good come out of Nazareth?" I was just like any other girl, learning to care for a home, walking with my mother as she carried the water jug from the well, ground the grain for bread, cared for our few animals. I anticipated being a mom myself one day . . . I'd marry of course and we'd live in Nazareth like my parents and theirs and theirs . . . and we'd have children . . . everyday life for everyday people.

But that all changed in a moment, in a split second, when I had a visitor. Me. Alone. Neither my parents nor family saw it. Nobody to corroborate my story. But it was true. A visitor . . . an angel . . he even had a name . . . Gabriel. How do I know? He told me! It wasn't a flash of light or a dream. I hadn't had too much of the wine my parents made from Nazareth's fruit. I was awake and clear . . . and amazed . . . I turned and he was there . . . "Greetings, you who are highly favored! The Lord is with you."

It shook me to the core . . . me? Favored? By God? I thought, he must have mistaken me for someone else . . . wrong house . . . wrong night . . . wrong girl. But Gabriel went on . . . and called me by name . . . "Mary . . . you have found favor with God." No mistake.

You've heard the rest of the story . . . the unimaginable happened . . . I was to be the mother of the Christ . . . the Son of God . . . and while my thoughts raced . . . the angel concluded by saying, "Nothing is impossible with God."

Afraid, amazed, humbled . . . I bowed and responded, "I am the Lord's servant. May it be to me as you have said." Me . . . the mother of the Savior . . .

My soul glorifies the Lord and my spirit rejoices in God my Savior, for He has been mindful of the humble state of His servant. From now on all generations will call me blessed, for the Mighty One has done great things for me—holy is His name. (Luke 1:46-49)

Solo: "Labor of Love," Andrew Peterson, © 2005, New Spring Music, Brentwood/Benson Pub.

Joseph's Heart

MALE READER *(reflective):* I am convinced that most men, perhaps every man, wants to have a son. Bravado? Perhaps. Or maybe that inner desire to pass on the heritage, the family name to yet another generation. I'll admit, there were times when I was alone in my shop in Nazareth, planing a piece of olive wood into a wagon wheel, when I would dream of having a boy of my own. Of course, I dreamed as well of a beautiful woman I'd take as my wife and the marriage we'd enjoy that would lead up to having that child and many others. My Mary . . . now there was a woman. Young, gentle, caring. We had great plans . . . plans for a home and a future . . . and a son.

So you can imagine just how difficult it was for me when she told me the news. I wanted to believe her. She had never been anything less than honest with me . . . but this was hard to swallow. She was with child . . . and it wasn't mine. You'd struggle too.

But then something changed all that. There was this one night . . . a night when I thought everything was falling apart. I tossed and turned, wondering just what I should do. Maybe a divorce was the only way . . . break off the relationship. But then, I found out that I wasn't alone in my room. I know it sounds crazy, but there was an angel there . . . an angel who knew me by name and knew my situation. He knew Mary and somehow he knew the predicament we found ourselves in. And what he told me changed everything. He said it simply . . . "Go ahead . . . take Mary as your wife. She is pure and the child within her is from God." And he told me more . . . what I was to do . . . he said, "You are to give that Child its name . . . Jesus . . . the Salvation of God . . . because He indeed will be the Savior who will bring forgiveness to His people."

I got up . . . and did exactly what the angel said. Wouldn't you? We proceeded with plans for our wedding . . . Mary became my wife.

And on another amazing night, this time in Bethlehem, I saw the face of the Child, Mary's son . . . *our* son . . . for the first time. And eight days later it was I, Joseph, who gave Him His name . . . I announced with both authority and humility,

"Our son will be called . . . Jesus."

Jesus . . . the Savior . . . *my* Savior . . . what an amazing name.

Solo: "The Name of Jesus", Edmond Lorenz, Public Domain

Gathered at the Manger

Reading of the Timeless Story: Luke 2:1-20 (KJV)

Congregational Hymn: "Hark! the Herald Angels Sing" (All three verses; all instruments)

Solo: "Wexford Carol", Mark Hayes © 2006, Lorenz Publishing Company

The Light of Christ Fills Our Hearts

John 1:1-14

SCRIPTURE READER: In the beginning was the Word, and the Word was with God, and the Word was God. He was in the beginning with God. All things came into being through Him,   and without Him not one thing came into being. In Him was life, and the life was the   Light of all people. The Light shines in the darkness, and the darkness did not overcome   it. There was a man sent from God, whose name was John. He came as a witness to   testify to the light, so that all might believe through him. He himself was not the Light, but he came to testify to the Light. The true Light, which enlightens everyone, was   coming into the world. He was in the world, and the world came into being through Him;   yet the world did not know Him. He came to what was His own, and His own people did   not accept Him. But to all who received Him, who believed in His name, He gave power to become children of God, who were born, not of blood or of the will of the flesh or of   the will of man, but of God. And the Word became flesh and lived among us, and we   have seen His glory, the glory as of the Father's only Son, full of grace and truth.

READER 1: The light has come. The Word became flesh and lived right here among us. Jesus. God with us. At last.

READER 2: We've gathered together for yet another Christmas Eve. We've anticipated this evening and tomorrow for weeks, perhaps months.

READER 1: We've heard the joyful songs of Christmas, been dazzled by the lights, chosen just the right gifts, and wrapped them carefully. We've waited and we've celebrated and we've worshipped . . . and it's been wonderful.

READER 2: But the message of Christmas doesn't get packed up by New Years and put in the attic with the rest of the ornaments and lights and wrapping paper. No, the joy of Christ's coming is just the *beginning* of the story. Emmanuel doesn't mean "God *was* with us" . . . it's the promise that He *is* with us . . . now and forever through the power of His Spirit.

READER 1: Beyond Christmas, beyond December, the joy of His salvation and the promise of eternity by His side . . .

READER 2: the forgiveness and grace we know because He came; the hope and joy and peace that Jesus alone gives is ours long after December slips away. God is with us. Hallelujah.

Music Ministry: "After December Slips Away", Bonnie Keene/Lowell Alexander © 1995 New Spring/Moltio Bravo! Music, Inc./Julie Rose Music, Inc.

Candlelight Carols

Words on screen

"O Little Town of Bethlehem" (Verses 1, 3, and 4)

"Angels We Have Heard on High" (Verses 1 and 4)

"Away in a Manger" (Verses 1 and 2)

"Silent Night" (Start with instruments then move to a capella; no words on screen)

Benediction

Lights up

WORSHIP LEADER/PASTOR: And now, may Jesus, the Light of the World, the Light that pierced   the darkness of history and the darkness of our own hearts, bring you His joy, His   presence, His peace as you celebrate His incarnation. Joy to the world, the Lord has   come! Amen.

Closing Hymn or Instrumental: "Joy to the World"

Postlude of Carols (Instrumental)

Scripts

The Days Are Coming

Arranged by Gordon Williams

Scripture References: Isaiah 7:14, 11:1-6; Jeremiah 33:14-16; Micah 5:2
(NIV, NRSV, NKJV, TLB, TM, and GNB)

Suggested Use: A Christmas choral reading for advent

Cast:

VOICE 1
VOICE 2
VOICE 3
VOICE 4
CHORUS

VOICE 1: The days are coming.

VOICE 2: The days are coming.

VOICE 3: The days are coming.

CHORUS: The days are surely coming.

VOICE 4: But you, Bethlehem Ephrathah, though you are small among the clans of Judah, out of you will come for me one who will be ruler over Israel, whose origins are from old, from ancient time.

CHORUS: The days are coming.

VOICE 1: "The days are coming," declares the Lord, "When I will make a righteous Branch sprout from David's line."

CHORUS: Behold, the days are coming.

VOICE 4: He will do what is just and right in the land.

VOICE 1: In these days Judah will be saved and Jerusalem will live in safety.

VOICE 2: This is the name by which it will be called; The Lord Our Righteousness.

CHORUS: The days are coming.

VOICE 3: Therefore the Lord himself will give you a sign: The virgin will be with child and will give birth to a son, and will call him Immanuel.

15

VOICE 4: God with us.

CHORUS: The days are coming.

VOICE 1: He will be great and will be called the Son of the Most High. The Lord God will give him the throne of his father David, and he will reign over the house of Jacob forever; his kingdom will never end.

CHORUS: The days are coming.

VOICE 2: A shoot will come up from the stump of Jesse; from his roots a Branch will be fruit.

CHORUS: A Branch of Righteousness.

VOICE 3: The Spirit of the Lord will rest on him.

VOICE 4: The Spirit of wisdom and understanding.

VOICE 1: The Spirit of counsel and power.

VOICE 2: The Spirit of knowledge and fear of the Lord.

CHORUS: And he will delight in the Lord.

VOICE 3: He will not judge by what he sees with his eyes;

VOICE 4: or decide by what he hears with his ears;

VOICE 1: but with righteousness he will judge the needy,

VOICE 2: with justice he will give decisions for the poor of the earth.

CHORUS: The days are coming.

VOICE 3: He will strike the earth with the rod of his mouth; with the breath of his lips he will slay the wicked.

CHORUS: The days are coming.

VOICE 4: The wolf will live with the lamb, the leopard will lie down with the goat, the calf and the lion and the yearling together, and a little child shall lead them.

VOICE 1: The days are coming.

VOICE 2: The days are coming.

VOICE 3: The days are coming.

VOICE 4: "The days are coming," declares the Lord.

CHORUS: Amen and amen!

The Tired Innkeeper

by Muriel Hemmings

Cast:
> INNKEEPER
> SERVANT BOY
> NARRATOR
> LOUD MALE VOICES

(A roll-away cot is on the platform. INNKEEPER *is lying or sitting on it.)*

NARRATOR: The keeper of the Inn undressed and tumbled into bed.
> He yawned before he closed his eyes and this is what he said.

INNKEEPER: I've been so busy all this day because of Caesar's tax.
> Folks swarming into Bethlehem leave no time to relax.
> Boy!

*(*SERVANT BOY *enters and bows.)*

SERVANT BOY: Yes, Sir.

INNKEEPER: I trust that no more travelers come.
> No customers desired,
> So don't you dare to bother me.
> I am so very tired.

BOY: Yes, Sir.

*(*BOY *bows and exits. Pause, then loud knocking is heard)*

INNKEEPER: Now who's that knocking at my door?

*(*BOY *enters and bows.)*

BOY: We have a problem, Sir. All the rooms are filled.
> Two travelers came. Vexed him, and pregnant her.

INNKEEPER: Take care of them yourself, my boy.
> I'm staying in my bed.
> I told you I'm too tired to move.
> Just send them to the shed.

BOY: Yes, Sir.

*(*BOY *bows and exits)*

INNKEEPER: Who what relief to rest my limbs
   when I can finally get precious sleep at last.
   No customers to see.

(*Pause. Again, knocking is heard*)

INNKEEPER: Now who's that banging at my door?

(BOY *enters and bows.*)

INNKEEPER: Boy, why disturb me? Why?

BOY: Some shepherds claim a host of angels
   fill the midnight sky.

INNKEEPER: What? Angels?
   Tell those stupid shepherds to
   Go back to their sheep.
   I'm going to scream in agony if I can't get some sleep.

BOY: Sorry, Sir.

(BOY *bows and exits*)

INNKEEPER: Sweet quietness! So good to rest.
   I've never felt so tired.
   If that boy wakens me again
   Immediately he's fired.

(*Long pause. Play quiet Christmas music. In the background . . .*)

LOUD VOICES: We've seen Him.
   We've seen Him.
   Oh what a wondrous morn.
   We've seen the Babe as angels said.
   A Savior has been born. (*Repeat*)

(INNKEEPER *sits with fingers in his ears and stamping his feet.*)

INNKEEPER: I've got my fingers in my ears.
   A Savior's born! Who cares:
   To wake me so some helpless child's
   Nativity is shared?

NARRATOR: And to this day some still ignore
   Good tidings angels gave,
   That Jesus, Lord of heaven, is born

   Our sinful souls to save.

The Joy of Christmas in Biblical Times

by Joanne A. Reisberg

Cast:

NARRATORS 1-16

ISAIAH—The Prophet

EMPEROR AUGUSTUS

INNKEEPER

3 MAGI

PRESENTERS—Non-speaking parts

BIBLE HOLDER

2 RAINBOW STREAMERS

TEN COMMANDMENT BEARER

2 WAVE HOLDERS

MOSES

MARY and JOSEPH

3 SHEPHERDS

2-4 SHEEP

STAR

Act 1

Scene 1

(First scene takes part in front of the curtain. All NARRATORS *and* PRESENTERS *line up off SR and enter on cue. Since each word is important, all words are spoken slowly and before a mike.*

Scene opens with NARRATOR 1 *and* PRESENTER *holding the large poster of a closed Bible, stepping out together. This format, with subsequent* NARRATORS *and* PRESENTERS, *is continued throughout. Each* PRESENTER *and* NARRATOR *exit stage following their part until Nativity tableau.*

Spotlight highlights NARRATOR *and* BIBLE HOLDER.*)*

NARRATOR 1: Our Holy Book of praise and laud, it holds, in script, the Word of God.

*(*BIBLE HOLDER *slowly opens the large poster size Bible. Exits)*

NARRATOR 2: This colored arc, a sign on high, became a covenant in the sky.

*(*RAINBOW STREAMERS *walk slowly across the stage holding all the colors of the rainbow in an arc. Exits)*

NARRATOR 3: These laws of ten, on slabs of stone, are rules from God for us to own.

(TEN COMMANDMENT BEARER *holds one large stone colored tablet in each hand and crosses stage. Exits*)

NARRATOR 4: He fought to set his people free . . . *(pauses for* MOSES *to lift his hands)* and raised his hands to part the sea.

(WAVE HOLDERS *enter SL dressed in black. They hold large blue waves together and when* MOSES *raises his hands, they part for* MOSES *to walk between them. All exit.*)

NARRATOR 5: Now hear our story, long foretold, as joyous words slowly unfold.

NARRATOR 6: Isaiah, the prophet, has news to tell of a Savior named Emmanuel.

NARRATOR 7: He speaks of One who'll soon be here to preach and teach and calm our fears.

ISAIAH *(enters SR wearing appropriate robe):* Messiah, the Christ, the Holy One, He's coming to earth as God's own Son.

Scene 2

(Curtain opens. SR spotlights EMPEROR AUGUSTUS *wearing robe. He holds scroll and slowly unrolls as he reads.)*

EMPEROR AUGUSTUS: Hark, my people. Listen to me. Register now. It's my decree. Throughout the hills of Roman land, I want a count. This, I demand. *(Rolls scroll back up and exits)*

NARRATOR 8: So Joseph traveled to Bethlehem; Mary, with child, did follow him.

(MARY *and* JOSEPH *enter SR and walk to CS. Stable off to the left, not yet highlighted)*

NARRATOR 9: The time drew near for the Baby's birth. The Son of God, coming down to earth.

(MARY *and* JOSEPH *together slowly walk toward the* INNKEEPER; MARY *stage-front.)*

INNKEEPER *(standing by pole stating "Inn"):* We have no room in the Inn ahead, but come, I will find a nice soft bed.

(INNKEEPER *motions them to follow toward a stable, SL. Door swings open to reveal a manger, two low stools.* MARY *and* JOSEPH *enter and sit. Baby Jesus in manger.)*

NARRATOR 10: In a manger now, the Infant lay, cooed to sleep by a bed of hay. A glowing light in circle form, was round our Lord when He was born.

(Spotlight on MARY, JOSEPH, and manger)

NARRATOR 11: At this same time, in the fields at night, men watched their flocks in the dim moon light.

(Robed SHEPHERDS enter SR with SHEEP—two to four children dressed in sheep costumes with ears—and motion for them to move across stage)

NARRATOR 12: Bright rays streamed down from heaven above, as angels tell of hope and love. Be not afraid, they sing with joy, then tell about the baby Boy.

(Spotlights shine on ANGELS dressed in white robes as they walk from SR.)

ANGELS *(in unison):* "For unto you is born this day in the city of David, a Savior which is Christ the Lord."

(SHEPHERDS listen to the ANGELS and go toward the stable.)

NARRATOR 13: The shepherds found the Son of God, and worshipped Him with praise and laud.

(Child wearing large white STARS in front and back of their body enters from back of the congregation and walks down the aisle toward the stage.)

NARRATOR 14: A star led men from far away to where the baby Jesus lay.

(Three MAGI follow the STAR; enter from back of congregation, moving toward stage.)

MAGI: These wise men three, astrologers, gave gold and frankincense and myrrh.

(MAGI hand their gifts to JOSEPH and one kneels before the manger.)

NARRATOR 15: Christ lives among us now each day. We know He hears us when we pray.

NARRATOR 16: The manger's real. He's born indeed! That all mankind can now be free.

(All cast members gather onstage to recite following lines.)

ALL: On Christmas night, let Christians sing, "Glory to the newborn King."

(End program with everyone singing first verse of "Hark! the Herald Angels Sing.")

Play

A Christmas Moment

by L. Ruth Carter

Running Time: Approximately 20 minutes

Themes: Faith, Comfort, Meaning of life, God's care, Miracles

Cast:

MARILYN—Middle-aged woman, professional photographer

ANNA—Owner of the café, older woman

SALLY—Teenaged waitress, Anna's granddaughter

Props:

ANNA

Tray holding a teacup

Small teapot

Plate with a muffin, milk, sugar, and napkins

SALLY

Cutlery

Menu

Second teacup

Small teapot

MARILYN

Handbag

Mail (including junk mail, bill, 2 Santa Christmas cards, family newsletter, and card with paraphrase of Psalm 30 as scripted)

Costumes: MARILYN should be dressed in festive reds and greens; ANNA should be dressed plainly with apron and hairnet; SALLY, simple uniform, but wearing a Santa hat or reindeer antlers, winter coat, and boots as called for.

Production Notes: This is a small café, two small tables with chairs. One table will be canted slightly to the right or left of CS, towards the side closest to the exit. That is where the action will take place. The second table will be USL or USR of the DS table, on the side farthest from the exit. Soft Christmas carols may be playing in the background.

(The room is empty. SALLY enters from the kitchen.)

SALLY *(looking around; calls out):* Grandma! There's nobody here. Should I start sweeping?

ANNA *(off-stage):* No, dear, I'll do that. But you can wash the tables again—just in case we get another customer.

(SALLY wipes a table, singing a popular Christmas song, dancing, wiping the table to the beat. Just as she really gets into the fun of it, she stops abruptly and stares off into space. ANNA enters with a broom. She picks up the song where SALLY left off. When she sees SALLY's forlorn demeanor, she puts the broom down and goes to her.)

ANNA: Honey?

SALLY: Oh, Grandma! For a minute there I was happy. Really happy.

ANNA: Yes. I was too.

SALLY: And then I remembered.

ANNA: And you stopped being happy.

SALLY: It wasn't that. I felt guilty.

ANNA: Guilty because you were happy?

SALLY: Yes.

ANNA: Your parents loved you. They would want you to be happy.

SALLY: But it's only been a year.

ANNA: A long, hard year. It's been hard for you, recovering from the accident.

SALLY: And look! I was dancing!

ANNA: And you felt guilty.

SALLY: Yes. And I thought, maybe I shouldn't go on the sleigh ride tonight.

ANNA: Sally, the loss of your parents is a wide, gaping hole for you. For me too. But remember—they wanted only the best for you. *(Grins)* For me too, of course, but mostly for you. They loved you. You were their daughter. You were very special to them. More importantly, you are very special to God—to the God they loved with all their hearts.

SALLY: I know all that, but . . .

ANNA: Yes . . . but. Sometimes knowing isn't feeling. Let knowing be enough for now. The feeling will come if you hold onto the knowing.

SALLY: I guess I'd like a message—a personal message from God that everything will be all right.

ANNA: I think you'll get one. *(Goes to the window and looks out.)* I thought I heard a car stopping. It looks like we've got a customer. *(Hugs SALLY.)* You're special to God, you were special to your parents, and *(picking up the broom, goes to the kitchen door)* you are special—very special to me. Now, look after our customer! And enjoy the sleigh ride tonight!

(MARILYN enters from "outside", SALLY picks up a menu from the far table and crosses to her.)

SALLY: Merry Christmas!

MARILYN *(a polite grunt):* Yeah.

SALLY: Table for one?

MARILYN: Yes.

SALLY: Over here. The crowd has pretty much left. And I do mean crowd.

MARILYN *(taking off coat, she hangs it on one chair and sits in the other):* Been busy, eh?

SALLY *(singing to the tune of "it's the most wonderful time of the year"):* It's the biz-busiest time of the year.

MARILYN: It's that, all right.

SALLY: Can I get you a drink?

MARILYN: A cup of hot tea would be nice. And a bran muffin.

SALLY: Coming right up. *(Exits)*

MARILYN: Perky little thing, dispensing all that Christmas cheer. *(Pulls a bundle of mail from her handbag and sorts it.)* Junk, junk, bill. Phone. *(Sighs)* It'll be a big one. Oh, good! Cards from the kids! Chuck'll be so pleased. *(Opens one. Santa Claus beams at her)* Santa. *(Opens the next. Another Santa)* Santa, Santa. Always Santa. And why not? Santa. *(A cry)* Oh, Chuck! Shy? *(Takes a deep breath and expels it gustily as she unconsciously pushes at the mail. Some of the junk falls to the floor. She doesn't notice. Says harder)* Why? *(Crumples one of the envelopes in her hand and almost whispers)* Why?

ANNA *(entering with tray holding the teapot, cup, muffin, milk, and sugar):* The great philosophical question of the ages.

MARILYN *(looking up, startled):* What?

ANNA: Here's your order.

MARILYN: Oh, thanks.

ANNA *(picks up dropped mail):* I think you dropped this.

MARILYN: What? Oh, yes. Junk mail. Just opening about a week's worth of mail.

ANNA (*holding up flyers*): Would you like me to file it for you?

MARILYN: Would you? Thanks.

(ANNA *puts mail in apron pocket, steps to second table taking rag from pocket and proceeds to wash already clean table.* MARILYN *has opened another card.* ANNA *nods at it.*)

ANNA: Nice to hear from old friends.

MARILYN: Yeah, sure. But do they have to write such long newsletters? (*Pulls out a newsletter filled with typing*) I'm too busy to read them all!

ANNA: Too bad we couldn't have them nicely spread out through the year.

MARILYN: That would be nice. We'd be able to savor each one.

ANNA: Do you write annual newsletters?

MARILYN (*wryly*): You got me. Most years. (*Falls silent*)

ANNA: But not this year?

MARILYN: Not this year.

ANNA: Nothing to say?

MARILYN: Not a thing.

ANNA: That was a pretty heavy "why" you were asking when I came in.

MARILYN: I guess so.

ANNA: Usually somebody who asks "why" like that has something to say.

MARILYN: Not me! (*Holds up newsletter, showing the printed side*): Once I would have written something like this. What I'm doing. What my kids are doing. My goals. Where we went for summer vacation. The new home we just bought. A job promotion. My husband's successes. (*A rather long beat*) All the same-old-same-old that I found so fascinating and had to inflict on all my distant friends and relatives.

ANNA: But not anymore?

MARILYN: Not anymore. (*Turns the paper over, showing the white side*) This is my life. (*Looks at it a little closer*) No, this . . . (*points to a small speck on the page*) this speck is my life.

ANNA: I can't see a speck.

MARILYN: Exactly! Why should I—what I do—what I want—make a difference?

ANNA: You don't think your life makes a difference?

MARILYN: It doesn't. The universe existed quite nicely without me for millions of years.

ANNA: Ah.

MARILYN: Cosmic reality will continue just as nicely without me when I'm gone.

ANNA: You're here now. That makes a difference.

MARILYN: Sure, I'm here. One life amongst billions. One heartbeat amongst . . . *(flings down the newsletter)* Oh, how can I expect to have any kind of significance? Any impact? Or even any moment?

ANNA: I don't know. Excuse me. *(Calling out)* Sally! *(SALLY enters.)* Bring me a cup, will you, dear? *(To MARILYN.)* Would you like a refill?

MARILYN: No, thanks. I've barely touched this. *(SALLY exits.)*

ANNA: Refills are on the house. So you have no significance? No impact?

MARILYN: And no moment.

ANNA: No moment? As in no import?

MARILYN: That's right. Absolutely none. No moment.

ANNA: What do you do?

MARILYN: That's what I mean! Nothing important! And even if I did do something deep and meaningful, what difference would it make?

ANNA: You mean in the scope of a vast universe?

MARILYN: You got it. I'm a photographer. *(Snorts)* A photographer! A recorder of moments.

ANNA: Maybe your pictures of moments will last beyond your moment.

MARILYN: Maybe. But how many pictures are there of sunsets and sea-scapes? Of racing horses or smiling brides?

ANNA: All of these are important to somebody.

MARILYN: How many photographs capture a child's wonder? *(Falters)* An old man's hope?

ANNA: Not enough. *(SALLY brings the tea to ANNA.)* Thank you, dear. Why don't you get ready to go now? I can finish cleaning up. Would you lock the kitchen door?

SALLY *(giving ANNA a quick hug)*: Sure thing. And thanks, Grandma!

ANNA: Enjoy the party. *(SALLY exits.)* She's got a do with her church youth group tonight she's been looking forward to.

MARILYN: Sweet kid.

ANNA: The best. So you take pictures of moments. I think everyone should have a chance to appreciate beauty. And to express it. You're blessed to have an art to do that.

MARILYN *(snorts):* My attempts at art are no better than anybody else's. These, too, shall fade away.

ANNA: Do they have to be better if they give pleasure to someone?

MARILYN: I'm a bit of a perfectionist. They've got to please me!

ANNA: You have family? A husband, children?

MARILYN *(nods):* The kids are all grown up and gone. They don't need me anymore.

ANNA: They will always need you, no matter how accomplished, how successful they are.

MARILYN *(not willing to concede):* Well, I guess . . .

ANNA: What about your husband?

MARILYN: Chuck? Chuck is . . . he's my best friend. An business partner. *(Picks up the Santa Christmas card)* The perennial Santa Claus.

ANNA: Santa Claus?

MARILYN: Yeah. We've been doing it for years. The mall management hires us to do the Santa photography. Chuck dresses up in his Santa suit and does the ho, ho, ho thing while I take pictures of the kids sitting on his lap. The crass commercialism of Christmas.

ANNA: They must be good pictures if they keep asking you back.

MARILYN: Naw. Lots of photographers can do just as well— *(wry grin)* or better. No, that's not why they keep bringing us back. It's Santa Claus.

ANNA: Chuck?

MARILYN: Yes, Chuck. He *becomes* Santa Claus, you see. In his heart. The children love him. He draws them to him—because *he* loves them.

ANNA: That's a special gift.

MARILYN: Yeah, it makes me fall in love with him all over again. To Chuck, each child is an individual, special. They sit on his lap and for that brief moment they are the only ones in his world. *(Eyes glistening as she feels again the magic.)* The pictures shine.

ANNA: And you say your life has no moment?

MARILYN: None!

ANNA: And Chuck? Does his life have no moment?

MARILYN: I didn't want him to do Santa this year. *(Getting lost in her thoughts, speaking more to herself than to* ANNA.*)* The chemo has been so hard on him.

ANNA: Oh, my dear!

MARILYN *(looking back at* ANNA*)*: He was all set to start radiation therapy when the doctors told him he'd have to stay away from children for a couple of days after each treatment. They said the radiation in his body would be too strong for kids, especially the small ones.

ANNA: Yes, I've heard that can be a problem.

MARILYN: The doctors said, "Wait for the kids."

ANNA: But Christmas won't wait.

MARILYN: No. He had to be there for the kids.

ANNA: What did the doctors say?

MARILYN: They didn't like it. They've got him booked to start just after Christmas, but they don't like the delay. I don't either. It might be too late. Too late for Chuck.

ANNA *(gently)*: But not too late for Santa Claus?

MARILYN: That's what Chuck said! Not too late for the children, he said. *(A whisper)* And never too late for a miracle.

ANNA: Not, it's never too late for that.

MARILYN: I wish I could believe that.

ANNA: You can't?

MARILYN: How can I?

ANNA: Because maybe that's sometimes all we've got.

MARILYN: What, miracles?

ANNA: No. Hope.

MARILYN: Hope. Hah. What good's that when all you can see is pain, suffering, and . . . *(stops abruptly)*

ANNA *(beat)*: But that's the point, isn't it? Hope shines brightest in the darkest night. That's when we need it most.

MARILYN: We don't need it when all it gives us is false expectations that get crushed time after time after time.

ANNA: True. That's why hope has to have a partner. *(Waits a beat, while* MARILYN *stares stonily at her)* Faith.

MARILYN *(sneers)*: Faith. That's no better than false hope.

ANNA: Unless we put our faith into something that's absolutely faithful.

MARILYN: I suppose you mean God.

ANNA: See! You do know the answers!

MARILYN: How can I? When today was just like yesterday and tomorrow will be no different?

ANNA: But today wasn't like yesterday, was it? *(More statement than question.)*

MARILYN: What? What do you mean?

ANNA: It wasn't. That's why you're here.

MARILYN: You mean—in this café?

ANNA: Yes. What happened today? Something, I'm sure, of *(a grin)* moment.

MARILYN: There he was, sitting on that big chair, with a long line of children to see him.

ANNA: Just like yesterday?

MARILYN: Exactly. And he didn't look anymore like Santa today than he did yesterday. Too thin, too gaunt. We had to pad his suit and buy a wig and beard. His voice isn't so hearty, either. But the kids keep coming. They remember him from previous years and they're eager to see him. They don't see the ravages of cancer.

ANNA: No, kids tend to remember the spirit of a person.

MARILYN: Yeah, and he's still got that. Even more so!

ANNA: He must be a wonderful man.

MARILYN: He is. My best friend.

ANNA: So you took pictures.

MARILYN: I could see his face getting more drawn as the day went on. But the children kept coming. He couldn't turn them away. His face was gray, his smile bright. Even in his fatigue, his eyes sparkled their delight with each child.

ANNA: Maybe he finds strength in their happiness.

MARILYN: Oh, he does. But still . . .

ANNA: I know. You're his wife. It's hard to watch your man suffer like that.

MARILYN: Not suffering. Nor really. Just wasting.

ANNA: Must be hard to concentrate on your own job.

MARILYN: Yeah. I took picture after picture until each child looked the same to me and I thought there never would be an end.

29

ANNA: What about today?

MARILYN: Today?

ANNA: Today is different, remember?

MARILYN: OK, OK. You're right. Today was different. There was Megan.

ANNA: Megan?

MARILYN: A little girl. Actually, I had noticed her because she waited so patiently, so quietly.

ANNA: A contrast to the other children?

MARILYN: Yeah, they were just having fun, but it gets so noisy sometimes. They run off and the parents yell. Some of them push a little, and cry if they think somebody else cuts in.

ANNA: But not Megan.

MARILYN: She just held her father's hand and stayed close to him. Such a solemn little face!

ANNA: She must have been adorable.

MARILYN: Wide, wondering eyes. She only looked at Chuck. At Santa. She didn't notice the laughter, the shouting, the commotion around her. She was intent only on Santa.

ANNA *(smiles):* I guess she had quite a list for him.

MARILYN: No, she didn't. She sat on Chuck's lap, told him her name and her age.

ANNA: How old is she?

MARILYN: Four.

ANNA: What did she want for Christmas?

MARILYN: Nothing.

ANNA: Nothing?

MARILYN: Well, no toys. Chuck does have to prompt the shy ones. He's so good with them! Not that Megan was shy. Just very, very focused.

ANNA: What *did* she want?

MARILYN: For her mommy to get better.

ANNA: Ah.

MARILYN: I started crying as I took the pictures.

ANNA: Cancer?

MARILYN: Yes. Megan told Chuck it's a bad disease. She was so earnest. It broke my heart.

ANNA: It's breaking mine.

MARILYN: Chuck just closed his eyes and held her close.

ANNA: The only real response.

MARILYN: She nestled against him. "Can you make her better, Santa?" she asked.

ANNA: My dear.

MARILYN: I know. Two big tears rolled down his face and he told her, "No, Megan honey, I can't make her better."

ANNA: There are no right answers, are there?

MARILYN (*shaking her head*): Megan was just asking what I've been asking for months. Make her better, Santa. Make him better, God!

ANNA: What did Chuck do?

MARILYN: He told her that he would tell his Boss.

ANNA: His Boss?

MARILYN: Yes. He said the Boss doesn't like it when people are sick. He said, "I'll tell my Boss about your mommy and He will help."

ANNA: Ah.

MARILYN: Chuck's with them now. He went with Megan and her father to see her mother in the hospital. He's going to introduce them to his Boss.

ANNA: His Boss. I'd never heard God described quite that way before. Does Chuck believe in miracles?

(SALLY *enters with her snow jacket and boots on. She hovers just inside the kitchen door, not wanting to interrupt the ladies.*)

MARILYN: Yes. Well, no. He doesn't believe in miracles, he says. He believes in the God of miracles. He won't put his trust in miracles. He'll trust in Jesus.

ANNA: What a wonderful way of looking at it.

MARILYN: Well, I don't see it!

ANNA: I don't understand.

MARILYN: I don't see how our puny little lives can mean anything to the Creator of the Universe!

ANNA: If you believe God can do anything . . .

MARILYN: But why should He? Megan has no more moment than Chuck or I do. Why in the name of heaven should He care? Why? Why?

(As MARILYN *rants, she's shoving her mail back into her bag, preparing to go. Some of the cards fall on the floor and* SALLY *moves in to pick them up. As she hands them to* MARILYN, *the top one catches her eye.)*

SALLY: Oh, my. May I? *(Reading aloud a paraphrase of Psalm 30)* "My child, I, the God of the Universe, Maker and Sustainer of all things, have lifted you up. Yes, you. You who cry and think you do not matter. You cried out to Me for help and I healed you . . . Sing, My child! Rejoice! My anger lasts for a moment. A moment, only. But My regard for you, My child, My love, yes, My deepest favour for you lasts a lifetime! A lifetime and beyond." *(She breathes a sigh.)* Oh.

MARILYN *(takes the card and continues reading, allowing the words to sink into her soul):* "Oh, My child, you weep now. Your weeping may last all night. But listen, My child! My joy comes in the morning. I turn your mourning into dancing. I take away your garments of grief and dress you in a radiant robe of joy. Be silent no more but sing! Sing My praises!"

ANNA *(looks up, smiling):* That sounds like a love letter to you. From your Boss. Merry Christmas, my dear.

MARILYN *(examining the card):* Why, that's a paraphrase of Psalm 30. The Bible.

ANNA: God's Word. And it's for you, just for you.

MARILYN: For me?

ANNA: Yes, for you. Your very own ray of hope. You see? You do have moment! *(This letter has a triple whammy as all three women take the message for themselves.)*

MARILYN: I have moment.

ANNA: Yes.

MARILYN: And Chuck. And Megan.

ANNA: And Megan's mom.

MARILYN *(whisper):* Yes.

ANNA: Merry Christmas.

MARILYN *(a deep shuddering sigh):* Merry Christmas. And thank you.

ANNA: You know Who to thank.

MARILYN: Yes, I do. *(Closing her eyes.)* Thank You, Jesus.

ANNA: Amen.

SALLY: Amen.